The Williams Sisters:
Venus and Serena

Mike Wilson

Published in association with The Basic Skills Agency

Hodder & Stoughton

A MEMBER OF THE HODDER HEADLINE GROUP

Acknowledgements
Cover: © *PA Photos*

Photos: pp. 8, 19, 22 © PA Photos; pp. 11, 24, 27 © AP Photos.

Every effort has been made to trace copyright holders of material reproduced in this book. Any rights not acknowledged will be acknowledged in subsequent printings if notice is given to the publisher.

Orders: please contact Bookpoint Ltd, 130 Milton Park, Abingdon, Oxon OX14 4SB. Telephone: (44) 01235 827720, Fax: (44) 01235 400454. Lines are open from 9.00 – 6.00, Monday to Saturday, with a 24 hour message answering service. Email address: orders@bookpoint.co.uk

British Library Cataloguing in Publication Data
A catalogue record for this title is available from The British Library

ISBN 0 340 84876 6

First published 2002
Impression number   10 9 8 7 6 5 4 3 2 1
Year   2007 2006 2005 2004 2003 2002

Copyright © 2002 Mike Wilson

Typeset by SX Composing DTP, Rayleigh, Essex.
Printed in Great Britain for Hodder & Stoughton Educational, a division of Hodder Headline Plc, 338 Euston Road, London NW1 3BH by Bath Press Limited, Bath.

Contents

1   The American Dream

A man stood in his backyard,
and looked around him.

He looked at his little girls.
Venus was five.
Serena was only four.
The year was 1985.

Richard Williams wanted the best
for his kids.
He wanted them to have a better life.

But they were poor,
and life was hard.

Richard Williams had faith
in the American Dream.
He had faith
his girls could get to the top –
at something.

But this was Compton,
the biggest ghetto in LA.
There were guns and drugs
and all kinds of bad people.

You had sport, and you had rap.
(Ice Cube and Dr Dre came from Compton.)

If you didn't have sport
and you didn't have rap,
there was no way out.

2 Power and Focus

Richard Williams was the son of
a poor farmer.
He ran a security firm in California.

In his spare time,
he was a tennis coach
for some of the local kids.
He read books on tennis.
He watched videos.
He knew a lot about the game.

He looked at his girls again.
When they grew up,
they'd be tall, fit and strong.

He got some tennis rackets,
and a supermarket trolley
full of tennis balls.
'Venus, Serena,' he said.
'Let's go to the park.'

Venus can remember the first time
she held a tennis racquet.

She was good at it.
She had power. She had focus.
She had drive.
She played on and on.
She didn't want to stop.

Dad went home and told mom:
'She's a real winner!'

Dad told Venus:
'You can go all the way –
right to the top!

'But you have to have faith in yourself.
You have to have faith in God.
And you have to work hard.

'But I know you can do it!'

Richard Williams knew that his girls could make it to the top.
Today they are stars, and even have dolls made of themselves!

3 Bullets Started Flying . . .

Soon Venus and Serena were spending
all their spare time in the park.
They had tennis practice every day.
Dad worked them hard.
But one day,
they got to go home early.

This is what happened:
The girls were playing tennis as usual.
A car pulled up.
They heard gun shots.
Bullets started flying.

It was a drive-by shooting –
pretty normal for Compton.

Venus and Serena got down on the ground.
They waited for the shooting to stop.
Pretty soon, dad said:
'Come on, kids. Let's go home.
We'll have to come back tomorrow.'

4   Prizes

Serena had her first big match
when she was four.

By the time she was ten,
she had won about fifty prizes.

The girls both went to
a tennis training school.
They met other girls there,
who would later be stars –
like Mary Pearce and Jennifer Capriati.

Jennifer Capriati trained at the same tennis school as
the Williams sisters.

Serena started making her living from tennis
when she was 14.

But her dad didn't let her burn out.
She had one big match in 1994,
three in 1995, five in 1996.
That way,
she kept up her school work.
Tennis wan't the only thing
in her life.

5   Just a Game

Venus and Serena have never let tennis
take over their whole lives:
'We also like going to the beach,' they say.
'We like just hanging out!'

Dad always told them:
'Tennis is just a game.
It's just chasing round after a little ball.
What's important is education.
Education is power.'

He made sure
his girls didn't forget their education.

Richard Williams on the training court with Serena.

Once, Venus's grades slipped.
Her dad slowed down her tennis training,
so she could work harder
at her school work.

Serena has won tennis matches
all over the world.
She has made thousands of dollars.
What does Serena say
was the best moment of her life?

Getting an A for Maths!

6 Staying Cool

Sometimes it was hard
for two poor little black kids
to fit in the rich world
of the tennis competitions.

'I won this competition,'
Venus recalls.
'I beat a white kid in the final.
I heard her dad say:
"How come you let that black kid beat you?
They're from Compton.
They don't even belong here . . ."

'I had to prove to them,' says Venus,
'that you can play tennis,
no matter if you're black or white,
rich or poor . . .'

Sometimes, the Williams family
still get comments like these today:

In California in 2001,
Venus pulled out of a big game
against Serena.
She had a leg injury.
Serena went on to win the final,
but the crowd thought it was a fix.

They thought Venus let Serena win.
So they jeered
and called Serena racist names.

The sisters both knew –
the best answer is just to stay cool.
Don't get angry.
Don't get violent
– and keep on winning!

7   The Will to Win

How could anyone think
Venus could fix a match?

In Venus and Serena,
the will to win is so strong.

Serena recalls:

'It really helps to have Venus watching
and supporting me.

'In one match I lost two match points.
I was losing it.
I looked up, and saw my mom and dad,
and Venus.
She was really there for me,
pumping me up.

'It really helped me!'

Venus says:

'In one match, in Australia in 1998,
I was watching Serena.
She was down 1–6, 0–5.
Yet she was still fighting.
It was like her life was at stake.

'I knew then,' Venus went on,
'I wasn't that strong.
I knew I had to be just as strong
as my sister!'

But that will to win can
stop you making friends . . .

One tennis star has said:
'Who does Venus Williams think she is!
She's so stuck up!
She's cut herself off
from the rest of us . . .'

Venus answers:

'I don't go to the big matches
to make friends.
I don't go to talk to people,
or go to parties . . .

'I go to play tennis,
and be the best!'

8   'We Never Fall Out . . .'

Sometimes the sisters
have to play each other
in a big match.

In 2000, they played in a semi-final
at Wimbledon.
In 2001, they played in the final
of the US Open.
Twenty-two million people saw it on TV.

Normally, Venus wins.
'I'm sorry I had to take you out, Serena,'
she said after one game.

So do they fall out then?
No.

Serena congratulates Venus on her win after their semi-final match at Wimbledon, 2000.

'We don't have rows,'
says Serena.
'The last row we had
was when I was about six.
It was about a toy, or something!'

'Serena can get upset if she loses,'
says her dad.
'Sometimes she cries . . .
but Venus just comes off court
and thinks about getting something to eat!'

9 The Fastest Serve

Venus and Serena also play together
in doubles matches:

In 2000, they won
the Wimbledon doubles title.
In 2001, they won
the Australian Open together.

They play mixed doubles too:

In 1998,
the sisters won all four Grand Slam titles:
Serena and her partner
won Wimbledon and the US Open.
Venus and her partner
won the French and Australian Open.

Venus and Serena with their doubles trophy at Wimbledon in 2000.

The sisters are just as strong
as the top men players.

In fact, Venus holds the world record
for the fastest serve by a woman:
A hundred and twenty-seven miles an hour!
That's faster
than some of the men players can manager!

10 More to Life than Tennis . . .

Venus and Serena live together
in a big house on Palm Beach.

Venus loves clothes.
She likes Calvin Klein, Moschino . . .
She loves the classic 1950s look.
She also designs her own clothes.

'I'll play tennis until I'm 26,' she says,
'Then maybe I'll work in fashion.
I'm just a beginner in the fashion world.
I've got a lot to learn.
But I'm getting there!'

Venus (right) loves clothes and would like to work in fashion one day.

For Venus, there is more to life than tennis.
Here are just some of the passions she has listed:

- sleeping
- shopping
- cooking
- beauty products
- playing guitar
- old English furniture
- roast beef and potatoes (no fad diets for her!)
- her little dog Bobby.

But there's no man in her life.
How come?

'I think people are so shy these days,' she says,
'and nobody wants to be rejected.'

Family is important to Venus and Serena. Here they are on a night out with their mom, Brandy.

Venus beat Serena
in the final of the US Open
in September 2001.
She won $850,000.
Serena won $450,000
for coming second.
But money isn't everything.

'I love you,' Venus told her little sister.

'I always want Serena to win,' Venus said.
'because I'm her big sister.
I have to look out for her.'

'Don't!' said Serena,
'you'll make me cry!'

'We've won a lot of big matches,
and we've won a lot of money.
But the best times
are when we win a doubles match together.
It's always such good fun!'

Tennis is just a game.
But a family is for ever.